LITTLE QUICK FIX:

UNDERSTAND PROBABILITY

#LittleQuickFix

Sara Miller McCune founded SAGE Publishing in 1965 to support the dissemination of usable knowledge and educate a global community. SAGE publishes more than 1000 journals and over 800 new books each year, spanning a wide range of subject areas. Our growing selection of library products includes archives, data, case studies and video. SAGE remains majority owned by our founder and after her lifetime will become owned by a charitable trust that secures the company's continued independence.

Los Angeles | London | New Delhi | Singapore | Washington DC | Melbourne

LITTLE QUICK FIX:

UNDERSTAND PROBABILITY

John MacInnes

SAGE

Los Angeles | London | New Delhi
Singapore | Washington DC | Melbourne

SAGE

Los Angeles | London | New Delhi
Singapore | Washington DC | Melbourne

SAGE Publications Ltd
1 Oliver's Yard
55 City Road
London EC1Y 1SP

SAGE Publications Inc.
2455 Teller Road
Thousand Oaks, California 91320

SAGE Publications India Pvt Ltd
B 1/I 1 Mohan Cooperative Industrial Area
Mathura Road
New Delhi 110 044

SAGE Publications Asia-Pacific Pte Ltd
3 Church Street
#10-04 Samsung Hub
Singapore 049483

Editor: Mila Steele
Production editor: Ian Antcliff
Copyeditor: Neville Hankins
Marketing manager: Ben Griffin-Sherwood
Design: Shaun Mercier
Typeset by: C&M Digitals (P) Ltd, Chennai, India
Printed in the UK

First published 2018

Library of Congress Control Number Available

British Library Cataloguing in Publication data

A catalogue record for this book is available from the British Library

ISBN 978-1-5264-5883-4

Contents

2 MIN

summary

Everything in this book!

Section 1 Probable events *may* or *may not* happen. Probable knowledge *may* or *may not* be true. Probability is important because all of science consists of probable knowledge. We *infer* the most probable conclusion given the evidence we have. But that conclusion *might* be wrong.

Section 2 We can calculate probabilities using trials, outcomes and sample spaces. A *trial* is any process whose *outcome* is uncertain, or any question whose certain answer we do not already know. In social science, experiments or social surveys are examples of trials. The *sample space* comprises all the possible *outcomes* of a trial.

Section 3 The trickiest part of probability is being able to see and analyse everyday life in terms of the probabilities. The secret is to see things in terms of trials and outcomes. After that, determining probability is just arithmetic.

Section 4 *Marginal probability distributions* sound technical but are just a way of describing how everyday things vary. Thinking about data in this way allows us to imagine the world as an endless array of trials with indeterminate but predictable outcomes. The addition rule allows us to understand these outcomes.

Section 5 When we look at the way probabilities join together, we can start to understand whether different social phenomena are related or not. They are a stepping stone to *conditional* probabilities. Conditional probability is a powerful way to describe how different conditions affect the probability of something happening. They bring joint and marginal probabilities together.

Section 1

The secret is to see everyday life in terms of trials and outcomes

Q

What is probability and why does it matter?

A

10 SEC summary

Probability uses a scale from zero to one to express how confident we are that something is true, or how likely it is that some future event will occur.

Probability is a scale between impossible and certain

Probability can be expressed as a proportion, fraction or decimal between zero (0) and one (1):

- zero means impossible or definitely untrue
- one means absolutely certain
- anything inbetween might happen or be true... or might not!

Probability is vital in the social sciences because free will makes social action and attitudes highly variable. Deterministic accounts of what must happen are implausible, so we explore what makes something more or less probable.

We also use probability because our knowledge is incomplete, may be mistaken or could be improved as more evidence turns up.

$0 < P < 1$

Probability describes anything that is neither impossible (P = 0) or totally certain (P = 1) as a proportion between zero and one. I'm a man. The probability that I'm pregnant is zero (impossible), the probability that I'm mortal is one (certain). The probability that the lottery ticket I've just bought will win the jackpot (in the UK weekly national draw) is about 1/14,000,000. The forecast tells me there is a 90% chance of rain tomorrow afternoon.

As well as describing what we expect in the future, we need probability to describe our knowledge of the present. For example, the probability of a board director of any of the UK's 100 largest companies being a woman was 28% in 2017, compared with only 11% in 2007. Social behaviour and belief display such enormous variation that the best we can manage is usually to describe what makes something *more or less probable*. Rarely can we formulate more deterministic laws. Even if we could, this would require us to reconcile them with human agency and free will. Men are more likely to be made company directors than women, but that means neither that no women are directors, nor that all men are!

HOW CONFIDENT ARE WE?

A forecast of a 90% chance of rain uses probability in a second way: to describe how confident we are about our knowledge, or any conclusion we draw from evidence. It doesn't mean that it will rain 90% of the time, or over 90% of the country. It means that the probability that a forecast of rain will prove correct is 90%.

DO IT YOURSELF

YOUR TURN

You know 10 things about probability already

We use the idea of probability all the time, usually informally and without being very aware of it. Write down as many words as you can that describe how (im)probable something is.

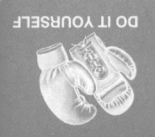

WHAT YOU KNOW ALREADY

DO IT YOURSELF

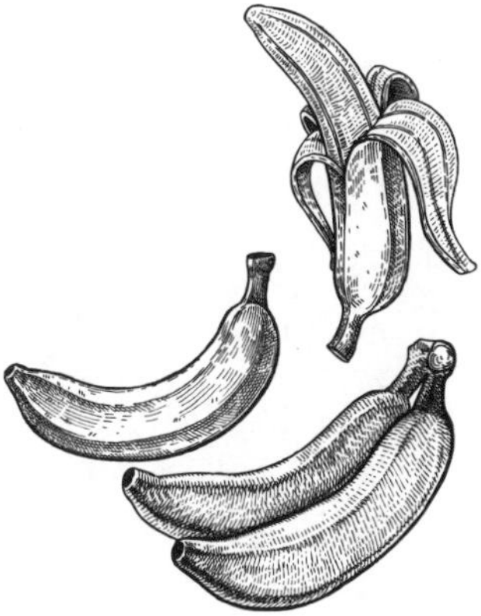

Probable answers

chance
hazard
danger
fortune
luck
risk
likelihood
prospect

odds
apparent
could
might
perhaps
possible
plausible
seeming

CHECKPOINT

Got it?

Q: What are the two main reasons for using probability calculations?

Got it!

A: To describe society, so that we can distinguish general features and trends from the wide variety of individual experiences.

A: To describe how confident we are about knowledge we think we have.

We can calculate probabilities using trials, outcomes and sample spaces

Section 2

Q

How do I work out how probable things are?

A

10 SEC

summary

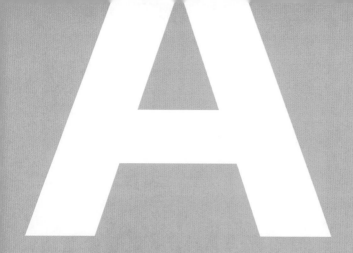

Probability can easily become confusing, so we use some very precise language: trials, random outcomes, sample spaces, series of trials and marginal probabilities.

To calculate marginal probabilities we define a trial and examine what happens when it is repeated many times.

A trial is any process that can have *more than one* outcome. Experiments, censuses, surveys, simulations and measurements are all collections of *repeated independent identical trials*. With a little imagination, almost any process becomes *a collection of trials*.

The list of *all* the possible outcomes of a trial is called the *sample space*. These outcomes must be *comprehensive and mutually exclusive*.

When identical trials are repeated many times as a series, *the law of large numbers* makes the frequency of any outcome compared with the total number of trials (its proportion) tend towards a limit which reveals its marginal probability.

Since each trial must have exactly one outcome, the sum of the marginal probabilities of all the possible outcomes *must be* one.

Fractions, decimals or percentages can all describe proportions and therefore marginal probabilities.

Trials must be *independent*: the outcome of each one cannot affect the outcomes of others in the same series.

TRIALS AND RANDOM OUTCOMES

To calculate marginal probabilities we think of a trial with two or more random outcomes. A trial is any process that creates an outcome or result. Random means not fixed or determined in advance. Some examples are:

- tossing a coin
- rolling dice
- taking someone's temperature
- sitting an exam
- recording whether a flight lands safely
- recording if a driver has a road accident
- recording data about someone (e.g., their age, sex, income, employment, view of capital punishment, etc.)

Random outcomes can be *events* (e.g., a coin lands on '*heads*', I *pass* the exam, the flight *crashes*) or *descriptions* (e.g., the temperature is *35.2*, my age is *92*). Experiments, censuses, surveys, questionnaires, records and measurements are all examples of collections of trials with random outcomes.

ALL THE WORLD'S A ~~STAGE~~ TRIAL

Almost any aspect of the social world can be thought of in terms of trials. My sex, age, address or how I vote look less random than tossing a coin, but this is only because these are all trials that have already taken place. Once a tossed coin has landed, the outcome is fixed. But what about the next toss? Similarly, until my conception occurred, neither my age nor sex was fixed. Neither was my vote until I cast it, nor my address till I decided to live there. Just as counting past coin tosses enables us to predict outcomes, so does collecting data on how people like me vote enable us to estimate what might happen in the future.

SAMPLE SPACES DESCRIBE EVERY POSSIBILITY

The list of all the possible outcomes of a trial is called the sample space. The sample space of a dice roll is [1, 2, 3, 4, 5, 6]. The sample space of a coin toss is [Heads, Tails]. The sample space of whether it will rain tomorrow where I live is [Rain, No Rain]. The sample space of the age of a person in years runs from zero to around 120. Outcomes in a sample space can be discrete categories [Heads, Tails] or continuous ones such as measurements of age, length, income, location or time. Outcomes comprising the sample space must be comprehensive and mutually exclusive. This means

- they must cover *every* possibility
- any individual trial can have one *and only one* outcome.

A tossed coin must land, and cannot land on both heads and tails on a single toss. A respondent must have an age, but cannot be two ages at once! Thus in any individual trial *something* must happen but only *one* thing can happen!

YOUR TURN

DEFINING TRIALS

Let's practice using the terms trial, outcome and sample space. These are words you should get used to using. Write down the sample space for each of the following trials.

Trial	Outcomes
Toss coin	______ ______
Roll dice	______ ______ ______ ______ ______ ______
The age of a person in years	______ ______
Driver's accident record	______ ______

Answers

Toss coin	Lands heads
	Lands tails
Roll dice	1
	2
	3
	4
	5
	6
The age of a person in years	0, 1, 2, 3,
	4, 5, 6, 7, 8…
	…98, 99, 100
Driver's accident record	Has had an accident
	Has never had an accident

Now try with real data

As you read in Section 1, the probability of a company director being a woman was 28%. What was the trial and what was the sample space?

....

....

....

....

Answers

Trial: What is the sex of this company director?

Sample space: [Man, Woman].

THE LAW OF LARGE NUMBERS

A single trial tells us little. However, the law of large numbers states that if *exactly the same* trial is repeated many times, the proportion of each outcome approaches a limit that corresponds to the underlying marginal probability of that outcome. The probability is the number, or *frequency*, of each outcome, divided by the number of repeats of the same trial that have taken place. To be identical each trial must also be *independent*: that is, its outcome must not be affected by the outcome of any other trial in the series.

CALCULATING P

The marginal probability, between zero and one, of any outcome within a trial sample space is given by

$$P = \left(\frac{\text{Frequency of the outcome}}{\text{Total number of trials}}\right)$$

With a coin. The proportion of times a coin will land 'heads' will approach 1/2 as the number of times it is tossed increases, even though it is common for such a coin to land the same way up many times in a row. We could say that the marginal probability of heads is 1/2 or 0.5 or 50%, or P(heads) = 0.5.

With dice. The proportion of times a die will land with a '4' up will tend towards 1/6 over dozens of rolls. The marginal probability of throwing a 4 is 1/6 or 0.167 or just under 17%, or P(4) = 0.167. The numbers look different but 0.167 and 17% mean the same thing.

Percentages are just fractions of one expressed in hundredths, so, for example, 95% = 95/100 = 0.95.

DO IT YOURSELF

COUNT LIKE A POKER PLAYER

There are 52 playing cards in a pack. There are 4 suits (Clubs, Diamonds, Hearts, Spades), 3 face cards (Jack, Queen, King) in each suit and 40 cards numbered 1 (the ace) to 10. We shuffle the pack well and pick a card at random (so that each card has the same probability of being picked). What is the probability that you pick...

A seven? ....

A Club card? ....

The Queen of Hearts? ....

Any face card? ....

Answers

1 There are four such cards, so the outcome 'seven' will have a probability of 4/52 = 1/13
2 There are 13 Clubs, so the outcome 'Clubs' will have a probability of 13/52 = 1/4
3 There is only one such card, so the outcome 'Queen of Hearts' will have a probability of 1/52
4 There are 12 face cards, so the outcome 'face card' will have a probability of 12/52 = 3/13

All the marginal probabilities of each outcome in the sample space must *always* add up to one as a total, because every trial has some outcome.

Coin toss: P(heads) + P(tails) = 0.5 + 0.5 = 1

Dice: P(1) = 1/6 + 1/6 + 1/6 + 1/6 + 1/6 + 1/6 = 1

Directors: P(woman company director) + P(man company director) = 0.28 + 0.72 = 1

NINE OUT OF TEN CATS

The law of large numbers has an amazingly useful consequence. Because it defines marginal probability in terms of proportions, we can flip between these two ways of describing things whenever we want. If nine out of every ten cats, or 90% of cats, or 0.9 of the cat population (proportions), have a tail, this is the same as saying 'the probability of a cat having a tail is 0.9, or 90%, or nine out of ten'. Note that this does *not* mean that every cat has 90% of a tail. It means that if we picked a cat at random, nine times out of ten, in the long run, we'd find it had a tail.

YOUR TURN

DO IT YOURSELF

In the Unites States, 1,920,718 students earned a Bachelors degree in 2016. Of these, 135,633 studied Social Sciences. What was the probability that a student studied Social Sciences?

Use a calculator or spreadsheet and work it out.

Answer

Total number of trials
(= total number of students) = 1,920,718

Frequency of outcome 'studied Social Sciences' = 135,633

Probability = 135,633/1,920,718 = 0.0706 = 7.1%

CHECKPOINT

List the essential characteristics of trials and sample spaces

Trial: ....

....

Sample space: ....

....

What does the law of large numbers state?

....

....

What must the probabilities of the outcomes from any trial sum to?

....

Answers

Trial: more than one outcome; outcome not determined in advance; can be repeated many times.

Sample space: lists all possible mutually exclusive and comprehensive trial outcomes.

What does the law of large numbers state? That in a large number of independent identical trials, the proportion of each outcome tends towards a limit that represents the probability of that outcome.

What must the probabilities of the outcomes from any trial sum to? One.

CHECKPOINT

The probability checklist

Check that you've understood the following

- [ ] Because of the law of large numbers, the proportion of outcomes in a long series of repeated independent identical trials will correspond to the marginal probability of each outcome in an individual trial.
- [ ] This means we can move between proportions and probabilities.
- [ ] Trials have outcomes described by a sample space, whose probabilities must add up to one.
- [ ] We can write down marginal probabilities as P(trial outcome) = number between 0 and 1.

Section

The secret is to see everyday life in terms of trials and outcomes

3

Q

What are the two essential uses of probability?

A

10 SEC summary

We *compare* probabilities to describe what events or processes are more or less likely.

We can also use probabilities to describe how probable it is a *future* event will occur, or that a statement is true, based on our past experience.

Probability is used to explain events in two key ways

Probabilities allow us to *compare* the likelihood of different outcomes, either from the same series of trials and sample space or from different series and sample spaces. For example, we've already seen that it's more likely for company directors to be men (0.72) than women (0.28), a comparison within the same sample space. We could also compare this with marginal probabilities of other kinds of professionals being women from different sample spaces, such as US Senators (0.21) or Heads of State (0.06). As we'll see in Section 5, we can also use conditional probability as a special kind of comparison when we have more than one series of trials on the same sample of people or objects.

We can also use probability to describe our *state of knowledge*, rather than describe the world itself, so we might describe ourselves as '90% confident' that a statement is true or that something will happen. However, we need to be careful about our language. *There is no statement that is 90% true, nor any event that 90% happens!* It is either true or it isn't; it happens or it doesn't. The probability refers to how sure we are about our statements or predictions.

This might look like having it both ways, but the law of large numbers comes to our rescue.

FIRST USE: COMPARING PROBABILITIES

Very meticulous records are kept of air passenger flights and road fatalities. Indeed the meticulous recording and investigation of accidents has turned civil aviation from one of the most dangerous ways of travelling early last century to by far the safest today.

We can treat each mile travelled by each car, train, bus or flight passenger as a trial with the two outcomes in the sample space [No fatal accident, Fatal accident]. We can total the passenger miles travelled by each method in any period, and the total number of fatalities recorded, so we have a series of trials for each transport type. To keep the numbers manageable we look at deaths occurring for every hundred billion miles travelled. For the United States in the first decade of this century the results are recorded in the table opposite. Cars are about a hundred times riskier than air flights.

Table 1 Deaths per hundred billion passenger miles (US 2000–9)

(passenger miles, US 2000–9)

Car	728
Ferry	317
Train	43
Subway	24
Bus	11
Flight	7

Let's consider this table and think about trials. What are the series of trials here? Remember that a trial = passenger mile travelled by one type of transportation.

Answer

Therefore, there are six separate series of trials.

YOUR TURN

Try the travel risk calculator

You've probably heard someone say that driving to the airport is riskier than flying on the aircraft. Is this true? Think about the probabilities of risk with the two series of trials (Car, Flight) and circle your answer.

Yes / No

Hint: look at the table on the previous page

Answer

Yes! But only if the length of your flight is less than a hundred times the drive to the airport. Remember: the trial was for each mile travelled. Flights typically travel *much* further than the drive to the airport.

WINNING THE LOTTERY, FALLING IN LOVE

Probabilities allow us to compare the likelihood of almost anything, from winning a lottery jackpot (in the UK, about 1/14,000,000 for each ticket bought) to being murdered (around 1/100,000 each year in Scotland), finding a job, becoming a student, passing an exam or falling in love. This makes probabilities fantastically useful in describing the world.

COMPARING OUTCOMES IN THE SAME SERIES

We've just compared outcomes from different series of trials. Sometimes, we just want to compare the outcomes from the same series. The next table is from a 2016 Pew Research Centre survey of US adults who were asked: 'In general would you say life in America is better, worse or about the same as it was 50 years ago for people like you?' The trial was repeated 1375 times. There were three possible outcomes in the sample space: 'better', 'the same' or 'worse'. Surprisingly, given that Americans were much better off in 2016 than 1966, many thought life was worse than before.

Table 2 View of life compared to 50 years ago

	P	N
Better	0.38	525
The same	0.13	183
Worse	0.49	667
All	1	1375

SECOND USE: PROBABILITY AS MEASURE OF UNCERTAINTY

What does a '90% probability of rain' mean?

Forecasts of one-off events still depend upon evidence from a large number of trials. If the forecast says rain in Tokyo is '90% likely' tomorrow, this may mean that 90% of computer simulations (trials) predicted rain (outcome) or that records of 90% of similar days in the past (trials) recorded rain (outcome).

Note that this does not mean that it is predicted to rain for 90% of the time, or over 90% of Tokyo. It means that there is a 90% probability of rain falling somewhere in Tokyo some time that day.

The next day turns out fine and Tokyo stays bone dry. Was the forecast wrong?

No! The forecast did not mean that rain *must* occur. That would be a probability of 100%. The fine day corresponded to the 10% of past rainless days, or 10% of computer simulations *not* predicting rain.

How lucky is my ace card?

If I draw a card at random from a pack of cards I don't expect to draw an ace: the probability of getting any other card is 12/13 or 92%. But if I do draw an ace, I don't conclude the probability is wrong or the pack is fixed. I've just been lucky.

In all these scenarios we use probability to describe how sure we are about something, when our knowledge isn't certain. It would be safer planning for rain in Tokyo than expecting an ace if I draw a card from the pack.

Evidence is about probabilities

Interpreting evidence from any kind of data uses both these applications of probability. We may have no interest whatsoever in how a specific individual voted, or their sex or age. However, we might be very interested indeed in whether women were more or less probable to vote a certain way than men, or whether age or other characteristics related to voting behaviour. We use probabilities to describe these patterns.

Random sampling and probability

We also use probability again to describe how reliable our results are likely to be if they come from a *sample*, making claims like 'We're 95% confident this is true.' For example, if we studied social mobility we'd never have the resources to follow the life course of every single child. Nor could we decide to study 'typical' or 'representative' children, since we'd have no way of knowing what *was* typical or representative. The ingenious solution to this problem is random sampling. *Little Quick Fix: Statistical Significance* deals with this.

Win–win? The key difference between one trial and many trials

Both our uses of probability might look as if we're trying to have it both ways and never be wrong. If it rains in Tokyo the forecast was a good one. If it doesn't rain, the forecaster points out how that was possible too! If I pick an ace I'm just lucky; if I don't, it's what I ought to expect.

The law of large numbers

This overlooks two things: the law of large numbers and the difference between a single trial and a series of the same trial. Unless the forecaster's predictions performed well, so that about nine out of ten times it actually did rain after a 90% forecast, we would no longer trust them. If I keep picking aces, I might want to check my pack of cards. The law of large numbers tells us that the forecaster should have a 90% success rate. Probabilities describe long series of repeated trials, such as 'days like this one', 'men', 'lottery tickets bought'. This allows the law of large numbers to kick in and we can start to make very accurate descriptions, despite the fact that individual outcomes are unpredictable and variable. Probabilities do not describe any single trial result, or individual population member. There is no such thing as '90% rain', something '95% true' or a company director who is 28% female. It either does or does not rain; something is or isn't true; a director is male or female. The probabilities describe the long run or overall balance of chances of each outcome.

Why probabilities hurt your head

Thinking about probabilities takes effort. Our brains seem evolved to produce causal explanations about the world around us using remarkably flimsy evidence. Telling ourselves stories about the world helps us to cope with a challenging and changing environment. Unfortunately these stories are usually comforting but wrong. To understand the world around us systematically we need to collect data. You may already have guessed where data comes from: data describes the outcomes from different series of repeated trials. The tool that connects data to probability is the *probability distribution*, which is what we examine next.

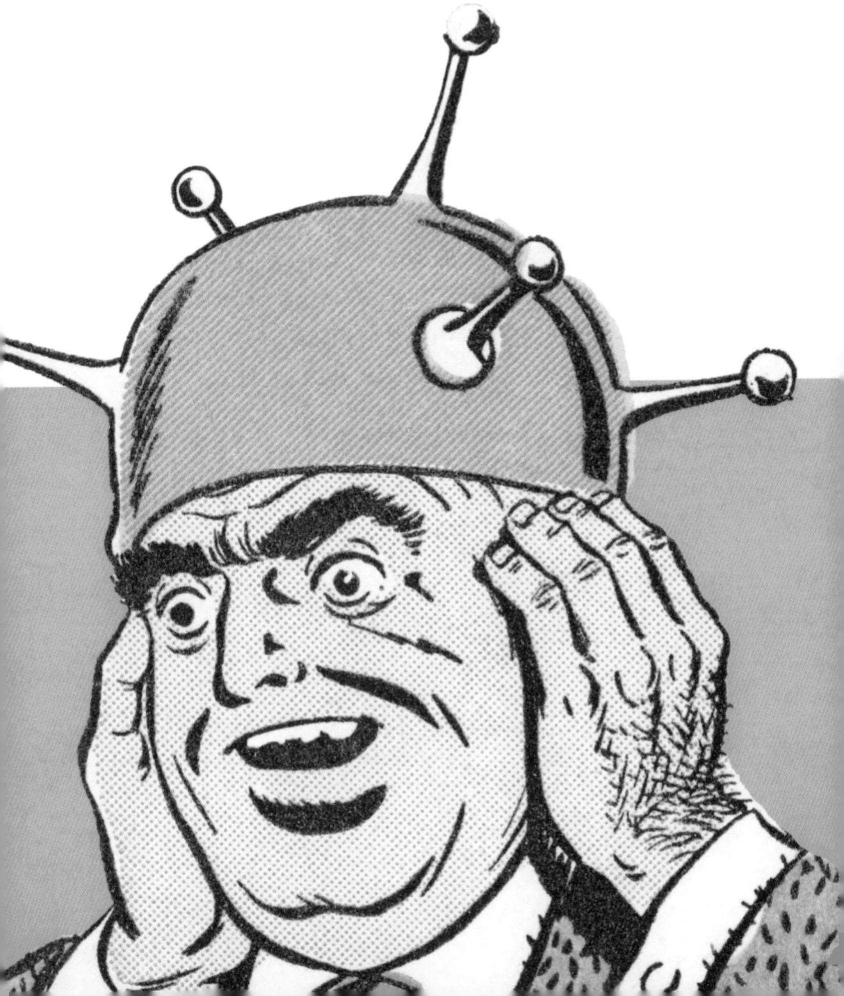

CHECKPOINT

We've seen two key uses of probability. Test yourself on each – if you can get these right, you're well on your way to understanding probability.

Comparing marginal probabilities between two different series of trials, or within one series of trials

In the current US Senate (2018) there are 100 senators; 21 are women, of whom 1 is African American. There are 2 male African American senators. If I pick a senator at random, what is the marginal probability of that senator:

Identifying as African American?

.... ÷ .... = ...

Answer: 2 + 1 ÷ 100 = 0.03

Being a man?

.... ÷ .... = ...

Answer: (100 – 21) ÷ 100 = 0.79

Being a man who identifies as African American?

.... ÷ .... = ...

Answer: 2 ÷ 100 = 0.02

CHECKPOINT

Describing how confident we are about our knowledge, or about predictions we might make

I've developed a new training technique to coach students through a national exam. I look at my records and see that for the last few years, nine out of every ten students using the technique have passed. How confident should a student be of passing the exam if they use the technique?

Answer

The law of large numbers suggests they should be 90% confident of passing. However, if we had more detailed records, we might well find that the pass rate differed between different kinds of student: more or less anxious, more or less studious, spend more or less time studying, and so on.

4

Imagine the world as an endless array of trials with indeterminate but predictable outcomes

4 Section

Q

How do probabilities add up?

A *probability distribution* shows marginal probability as a table or bar chart. This is a powerful way of understanding any data.

A probability distribution shows the number of times or frequency that each result has occurred within a series of trials. *Frequency tables* and *bar charts* show *probability distributions*. Since every trial has a single result, the frequency of each result must correspond to the proportion of trials having that result and therefore the probability of that result.

If the probability of any outcome plus the probability of all the other outcomes equals one, then the probability of any individual outcome must also equal one minus the probability of all the other outcomes:

P(outcome) = 1 – P(all other outcomes)

P(not that outcome) = 1 – P(outcome) = P(all other outcomes)

It must therefore also follow that the probability of any one of a number of outcomes is the sum of their individual probabilities:

P(A or B) = P(A) + P(B)

where outcomes A and B are from the *same* sample space.

Both these addition rules are much easier to follow using some real data. Let's do that now.

(Do people feel) LIFE IS GETTING BETTER?

Table 2 on page 48 was a *marginal probability* distribution. It shows the distribution of the probabilities of each outcome in the sample space. Remember: we can move between proportions or probabilities and percentages by multiplying by 100, as I've done in Table 3. Pictures are good ways to convey information. We can turn the table into a bar chart with the height of the bars representing the marginal probabilities, as in Figure 1.

Table 3 View of life compared with 50 years ago

	%	N
Better	38	525
The same	13	183
Worse	49	667
All	100	1375

Figure 1 View of life compared with 50 years ago

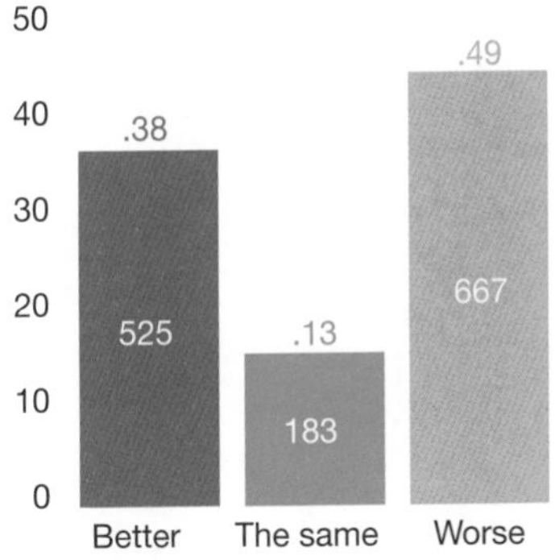

We saw in Section 2 that the probabilities of all the possible outcomes in a series of trials must total one. Frequency tables and bar charts show probability distributions:

$$\begin{aligned} P(\text{better}) + P(\text{the same}) + P(\text{worse}) &= 0.38 + 0.13 + 0.49 \\ &= 1.0 \end{aligned}$$

If we can add probabilities this way, it must also work for different combinations of outcomes. So the probability of thinking life is *either* the same *or* worse must be

$$P(\text{the same}) + P(\text{worse}) = 0.13 + 0.49 = 0.62$$

If the sum of all probabilities is one, then the probability of any individual outcome must be the same as one minus the total of all the other outcomes:

$$\begin{aligned} P(\text{better}) &= 1 - (P(\text{the same}) + P(\text{worse})) \\ &= 1 - (0.13 + 0.49) \\ &= 1 - (0.62) \\ &= 0.38 \end{aligned}$$

DO IT YOURSELF

YOUR TURN

Practise with some real data

Table 4 Does anyone in the household own a gun?

	%	N
The respondent *only*	23	306
Other household member(s) *only*	14	185
Respondent *and* other household member(s)	15	190
***No one* in the household**	48	627
All	100	1308

We'll use this data, which came from the same survey, to make some statements about gun ownership. Use the addition rules we've just looked at to work out the following probabilities:

Probability that someone owns a gun

.... + ... = ...%

Answer: 23 + 15 = 38%

Probability someone lives in a household where someone owns a gun

.... + ... + ... = ...%

Answer: 23 + 14 + 15 = 52%

Probability that someone does not own a gun

.... + ... = ...%

Answer: 14 + 48 = 62%

Or we could use the first probability we worked out, that is

.... – .... = ...%

Answer: 100 – P(owns a gun) = 62%

Now, when you see a bar chart or table, you can turn it from a description of proportions – 'nine out of ten cats have tails' – into a statement of probabilities – 'any cat has a 90% chance of having a tail'

CHECKPOINT

When I describe each of the probabilities obtained in a series of trials, what do I produce? ....

Answer: A marginal probability distribution

What are good ways to display this? ....

Answer: A frequency table, a bar chart

What rule does this use?

....

....

....

Answer: The addition rule:

P(outcome A) + P(outcome B) = P(outcome A or B)

P(outcome A) + P(all other outcomes) = 1

Section 5

Conditional probability describes how different conditions affect the probability of something happening

Q

How do conditional probabilities describe social relations?

A

Conditional probability tells us what conditions might make something more or less likely – essential in social science!

Earlier we saw that probability can describe social processes without being deterministic or overpowering the variability of social relations. We can do this best by exploring whether different *conditions* make things more or less probable. We can explore what *conditions* make belief in progress, or gun ownership, or women company directors, or any other social fact more or less probable. Conditional probability thus allows us to describe and explore social relations.

In Section 1 we saw that 28% of company directors were women. You understood what this meant: that, for whatever reason, men have been far more likely to end up as company directors than women; 28% was a conditional probability. In other words, the probability of being a woman, *conditional upon* being a company director, or *given that* the person was a company director, was 28%.

More precisely, we can use the language of trials. When we have two or more different series of trials *on the same subjects*, we can examine both marginal probabilities and conditional probabilities.

CONDITIONAL PROBABILITY AS A CONTINGENCY TABLE

Earlier we saw that many Americans seem pessimistic about progress. Using conditional probability, we can explore what is associated with these views. 'Born-again' evangelical Christians are often upbeat. Are they more optimistic about progress?

Table 5 shows respondents' view of life is conditional upon whether they described themselves as 'born again'. The probabilities are represented as percentages.

In the body of the table (in **green**), if we read down the columns we have the probability of thinking life is better or worse, conditional upon being 'born again' or not. There are two conditional probability distributions, one for those who are 'born again' and one for all other respondents. By comparing the columns side by side we can see that while evangelicals think it has got worse by a majority of about two to one (59% versus 29%), others are split fairly evenly. Therefore we can say that respondents' view of life was *conditioned by or associated with* whether or not they were 'born again'. Evangelicals are actually more pessimistic about progress.

Table 5 View of life compared with 50 years ago by religion

Column %	Born again	Other	All
Better	29%	43%	38%
	141	384	525
The same	12%	14%	13%
	56	126	182
Worse	59%	43%	49%
	284	383	667
All	100	100	100
	481	893	1374
	(35%)	(65%)	

You can see in the table two other probability distributions in the margins (in red). The far right-hand column contains the marginal probability distribution for view of life (regardless of whether or not respondents were born again) and the bottom row contains the marginal distribution for whether respondents were *born again* (regardless of what their view of life was). Now you know why single probability distributions are called *marginal* distributions!

Reading contingency tables

Contingency tables like this hold a lot of information, which is why they are so useful. In fact there is a third set of probabilities lurking in the table: the *joint* probabilities of view of life *and* being born again.

These describe the probability of each combination of outcomes from our two series of trials. You can see in each cell of the table the number of outcomes for each combination below the conditional probability percentage. Thus, for example, there were 141 respondents who were born again *and* thought that life was better now compared with 50 years ago. Dividing these numbers by the total number of trials (1374, shown at the bottom right of the table) gives us the joint probabilities.

DO IT YOURSELF

PRESIDENTS AND GUNS

The Pew survey we saw earlier also asked how people would vote in the US Presidential election

Was support for Trump conditioned by gun ownership?

Table 6 Voting intention by gun ownership

Support	**Gun owner?**		
	Yes	**No**	**All**
Clinton	32%	67%	54%
	168	575	743
Trump	68%	33%	46%
	353	279	632
All	100	100	100
	521	854	1375
	(38%)	(62%)	

You can see two other probability distributions in the table margins

WHAT DO YOU THINK?

DO IT YOURSELF

☐ **Yes**, there is a strong link – gun ownership makes a difference

or

☐ **No**, there isn't a strong link – gun ownership didn't influence voter support

It looks like there is a strong link. The probability of being a Trump supporter, conditional upon being a gun owner, was 68%, whereas only 33% of those without guns supported him. I could summarise the table in other ways too. I could say gun owners were twice as likely to support Trump as Clinton, while for those without guns the opposite was true.

Some useful notation

A quick way to write down conditional probabilities is to use a vertical line '|'. Thus P(Trump | Gun) is a quick way of writing 'the probability of supporting Trump, conditional upon owning a gun'.

PRESIDENTS AND PROGRESS

Here is a contingency table for view of life conditional on how respondents said they would vote in the presidential election. Use the raw numbers in each cell of the table to work out each conditional probability. Find the percentage in each table cell by dividing the number of outcomes it contains by the total number of trials found in the margin at the bottom of the table column. Some cells have been filled in to show you how.

Table 7 View of life by voting intention

Column %	Clinton	Trump	All
Better	436/716 = 60.9% 436	 89	38.2% 525
The same	 131	52/659 = 7.9% 52	13.3% 183
Worse	149	518	48.5% 667
	716	659	1375

WHAT DO YOU THINK?

DO IT YOURSELF

Use your table to answer these questions:

You can read this as 'what is the probability that Trump supporters think life is getting worse?'

What was P(Worse | Trump)?

= 518/659 = 78.6%

What was P(Worse | Clinton)?

= 149/716 = 20.8%

And now you can read this too!

What does this tell you about why Trump's campaign slogan was 'Make America Great Again'?

....

....

....

....

CORRELATION IS NOT CAUSATION

A large majority of Trump supporters think life has worsened, while the reverse is true for Clinton. Note that association or correlation doesn't mean cause. Perhaps believing that America needs to become 'great again' encourages people to think that life is worse for them. Or perhaps people who think life is getting more difficult, find that message appealing. Both are plausible and consistent with our evidence.

CAUTION

P(A | B) is *not* the same as P(B | A). Do not confuse row percentages and column percentages.

P(View of life | Voting intention) is the probability of being optimistic or pessimistic conditional upon being a Trump or Clinton supporter. However, if we ran the probabilities or percentages along the table rows instead of down the columns we'd get P(Voting intention | View of life): whether someone was more or less likely to vote for each candidate, conditional upon whether they were optimistic or pessimistic. It tells the same story but in a different way.

Table 8 Voting intention by view of life

Row %	Clinton	Trump	All
Better	83.0% 436	17.0% 89	38.2% 525
The same	71.6% 131	28.4% 52	13.3% 183
Worse	22.3% 149	77.7% 518	48.5% 667
	52.1% 716	47.9% 659	1375

PRESIDENTS AND CITIZENS

US presidents must be 'natural born citizens' of the United States. Therefore the probability of being a natural born citizen (A), conditional upon being president (B), is one. Conversely the probability of being president conditional upon being a natural born citizen is around 0.000000003. P(citizen | president) is not the same as P(president | citizen).

Independence

How do things look when one probability is *not* conditional on another?

Table 9 shows the probability of being born again, conditional upon sex.

Table 9 Sex and religion

Religion	Sex		
	Male	Female	All
Born again	35%	35%	35%
	224	252	476
Others	65%	65%	65%
	422	477	899
All	100	100	100
	646	729	1375
	47%	53%	

When you compare the conditional probabilities along the rows of the table they do not change, and both the conditional probability distributions are the same as the marginal probability distribution for being born again 'unconditioned by sex'. If the conditional probabilities do not change then *there is no association*, or we can say that the two probability distributions are independent of each other.

A LAST GAME OF CARDS

There is one final neat result to see, but to understand it properly let's do a final bit of card shuffling. Imagine you draw a card at random from a pack. You put the card back, shuffle thoroughly and repeat. There are 26 red and 26 black cards in a pack, so the probabilities must look like this 'tree' diagram

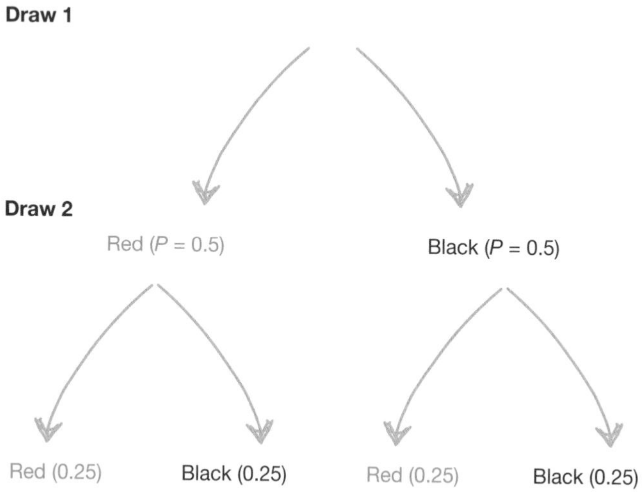

On each draw you have a 50% chance of getting a red card. So the chances of getting red cards on both draws must be $0.5 \times 0.5 = 25\%$ or 1 in 4. This experiment could be extended by adding further rounds of shuffles and draws. Each extra 'round' would double the number of possible combinations of results. It would follow that the probability of obtaining any single combination of results would decrease by half. Thus the probability of three red cards would be 0.125, of four reds 0.0625, and so on.

I can make these calculations only because I know that *the pack of cards has no memory*. Picking a red card on one draw has no possible effect on the colour of the card I pick in the next draw, as long as I've shuffled the cards properly. Because of this there can be no possibility of the probability of picking a red card on one draw being conditional upon which colour of card I drew in the previous round. Because the probabilities don't affect each other, I can multiply them together to get joint probabilities.

The fact that cards, dice, roulette wheels or tossed coins have no memory explains ' the gambler's fallacy'. People tend to believe that a run of black cards or 'heads' or even numbers ought to make a red card or 'tail' or odd number more likely to turn up next time, to 'even things out'. Casinos make a lot of money from this belief! If I have a fair coin, and toss it, how it lands next time can have nothing to do with how it has landed in the past.

This thought experiment gives us a useful conclusion:

- *If* two series of trials are *independent, then* we can calculate the joint probability of each outcome by multiplying together the *marginal* probabilities of each trial series.

We can also describe our conclusion in another way by reversing its logic:

- *If* we can calculate the joint probability of each outcome by multiplying together the marginal probabilities of each trial series, *then* the two series of trials are *independent*.

Now go back to Table 9 on sex and religion. You'll find the same rule works here, because there is no association between sex and whether or not someone thought of themselves as born again. You can check this by multiplying the number of outcomes in the margins of the table corresponding to each cell, and dividing the result by the total number of trials (1375). The results will be very close to the numbers found in each cell of the table:

$$
\begin{aligned}
P(\text{male}) \times P(\text{born again}) &= 646 \times 476/1375 \\
&= 307{,}496/1375 \\
&= 223.6
\end{aligned}
$$

$$
\begin{aligned}
P(\text{male}) \times P(\text{other}) &= 646 \times 899/1375 \\
&= 580{,}754/1375 \\
&= 422.4
\end{aligned}
$$

$$
\begin{aligned}
P(\text{female}) \times P(\text{born again}) &= 729 \times 476/1375 \\
&= 347{,}004/1375 \\
&= 252.42
\end{aligned}
$$

$$
\begin{aligned}
P(\text{female}) \times P(\text{other}) &= 729 \times 899/1375 \\
&= 655{,}371/1375 \\
&= 476.6
\end{aligned}
$$

This gives us the *multiplication rule* for probability:

If two series of trials A and B are independent, then
P(A and B) = P(A) × P(B)

HOW DO MARGINAL, JOINT AND CONDITIONAL PROBABILITIES FIT TOGETHER?

Marginal, joint and conditional probabilities are all related to each other.

You may come across this intimidating looking formula for conditional probability:

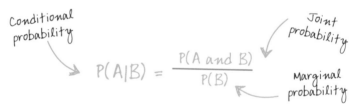

Conditional probability → $P(A|B)$; Joint probability → $P(A \text{ and } B)$; Marginal probability → $P(B)$

$$P(A|B) = \frac{P(A \text{ and } B)}{P(B)}$$

Don't let it scare you! The formula says the probability of A *conditional* on B equals the *joint* probability of A *and* B, divided by the *marginal* probability of B. It might look complicated at first, but actually it describes what you have already done if you've followed the exercises.

In everyday language it just says, ‘Considering only what happens when B is true, what is the probability of A being true?’ Or using the language of proportions, ‘What proportion of all Bs are also As?’

It describes the columns of the tables we’ve examined in this section.

WHAT THIS MEANS FOR SOCIAL SCIENCE

Because it reveals *associations* between different marginal probability distributions, conditional probability is a fundamental building block of every piece of social science that uses empirical evidence.

If something is not conditional upon something else, we can multiply probabilities together to get the joint probability of both things being true.

Once we can tabulate which conditions are associated with raising or lowering the probability of any feature of social life, we can describe, understand and explain almost any feature of society.

To make sure you have mastered all you need to know about probability, here's a final checklist. Check that you can now...

- [ ] describe a trial in terms of the sample space and its comprehensive and mutually exclusive outcomes
- [ ] calculate the marginal probability distribution from any series of trials or collection of data
- [ ] move between probabilities, proportions and percentages using the law of large numbers
- [ ] understand the two uses of marginal probability distributions

HOW TO KNOW YOU ARE DONE

CHECKPOINT

- [ ] calculate the joint probabilities for two marginal probability distributions
- [ ] compare the empirical joint probabilities with the expected probabilities to see if two marginal probability distributions are independent
- [ ] calculate conditional probabilities and use them to describe any relationship that exists between a condition and a marginal probability distribution

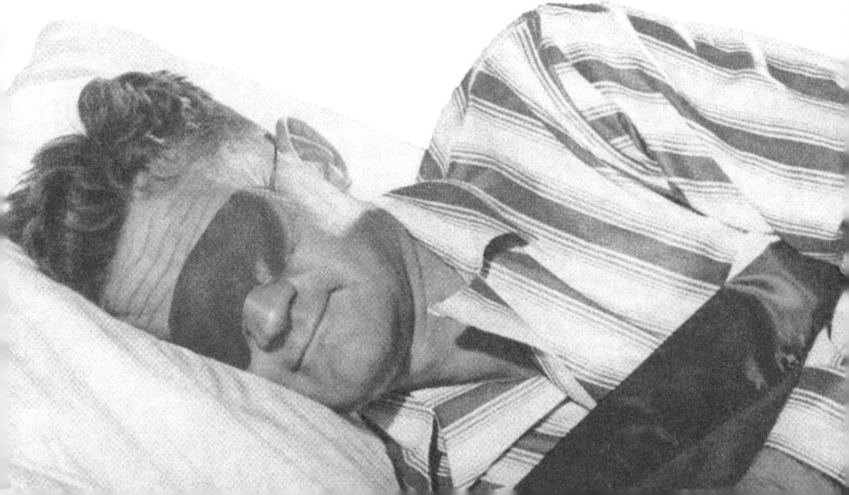

Glossary

Association Exists when two variables or probability distributions which are *not* independent of each other.

Bar chart Graph of horizontal or vertical bars proportional in length to the frequencies in a table.

Causation Process where prior occurrence of an event or condition increases the probability of another event or condition.

Column percentage Count in a contingency table cell expressed as a percentage of the total count in that table column.

Comprehensive and mutually exclusive *See* mutually exclusive and comprehensive.

Conditional probability $P(A|B)$ = the probability of A, given, contingent upon, conditional upon, conditioned on, or dependent upon B occurring or being true.

Contingency table The probability distribution for a set of trials, conditional upon another set of trials.

Empirical based on some form of measurement.

Expected joint probability P (A) * P(B) = when two marginal probability distributions are independent their joint probability is the product of the two distributions.

Fair Unbiased.

Frequency The number of times an outcome occurs in a set of trials.

Frequency table A table of a marginal probability distribution.

Gambler's fallacy The failure to see that in a series of independent repeated trials, the results of one trial or series of trials cannot affect the results of any other trial.

Independence Two probability distributions are independent when they are not associated, so that P(A|B) = P(A).

Infer Draw conclusions from empirical evidence.

Joint probability The probability of both A and B occurring or being true; *see also* expected joint probability.

Law of large numbers In a very long run of identical independent repeated trails, the proportion of each outcome tends towards a limit corresponding to its underlying probability.

Marginal probability A probability distribution from one set of trials, as displayed in the margins of a contingency table.

Mutually exclusive and comprehensive Outcomes in a sample space must cover every possibility, and the result of every trial can be assigned to only one outcome.

N, n The total number of trials or outcomes or observations.

Outcome The result of a trial.

Probability distribution The distribution of all outcomes from a set of trials.

Proportion Fraction of a whole number.

Random Undetermined.

Row percentage Count in a contingency table cell expressed as a percentage of the total count in the table row.

Sample space The set of all possible mutually exclusive outcomes from a trial.

Table body The cells within a contingency table, excluding the marginals.

Table margin The row distribution to the right of, and column distribution below, the body of a contingency table.

Tree diagram The pattern of outcomes from two or more trials.

Trial A process which results in only one of at least two possible outcomes.